Human Resources

Human Resources

Jesse Waters

INK
BRUSH
PRESS

ISBN 978-0-9827514-6-6
Library of Congress Control Number: 2010942761

Cover photograph by Randy Edwards
Book design by Ashlynn Ivy

Ink Brush Press
Temple, Texas
www.inkbrushpress.com

Acknowledgments

Adirondack Review: "When I Need a Moment" (originally "Something to be Said for Self-Gratification"), "To A Young Couple Planning Their First Vacation, Thinking of Divorce" and "Take All the Time"

Cimarron Review: "Observations during a Flat Tire Repair Across the Street from PS 39 Elementary, New York, NY"

Coal Hill Review: "What the Sous Chef Knows"

Concrete Wolf: "Tilt-A-Whirl" (originally "Magnetics")

The Cortland Review: "You Are Here" (originally "Each Beginning Is the Furthest Thing")

88: A Journal of Contemporary Poetry: "Swine Logic," "The Problem with Crumbs,"and "A New Walk"

Magma: "Metropolitan Heart"

Plainsongs: "My Father Teaches Me What it Means to Burn"

Poetry Quarterly: "Adam's Blues"

River Styx: "Working All the Angles"

Sycamore Review: "Roast"

I truly appreciate the editors of the magazines who originally published these poems. I'm also appreciative of the Vermont Studio Center and North Carolina Arts Council for the time and support that helped make this book possible.

I'm grateful to the following artists for their occasional suggestions, ata-boys, eye-rolling, wine-sharing and/or direction as I wrote these poems: Kathleen Halme, Mark Cox, Richard Jackson, Julianna Baggott, Bruce Weigl, Mike White, Robb Kunkel, Jill Rosser and Billy Collins.

For Karen, and Harold and Laura

Human Resources

Compliance and Liability

New Transfer

Family Business

Over Time

Skill Set

Compliance and Liability

Adam's Blues

A woman can get the hair
away from her own face, but
she'd rather you used your hand.

She can zip up the back
of her own black dress—still,
trust this—she'd rather you used your hand.

Most women can check
their own hearts with that stethoscope, yet
they love it when the hand is cupped

familiar against her rib. Shoot
her own shit, pay her own freight,
break boards in half, co-sign. Dig graves.

No one saves themselves from drowning.
Use your hand to cut the deck
in half and double-down. Alone in the den

I may drink my late tea laced,
but even I know that a woman
wants hand—that indifferent limb at my silent

side—to take both blame and blossom
just once this time, and pick that fruit myself.
She's already got my world in just the love line

of her juice-stained palm.

Tailor Made

In my den drinking dark tea
laced with obsessions, I watch a lot of late night television:
Kermit the Frog and Miss Piggy—
what's the deal with that? Forget
science, forget architecture of bodies—
their relationship throws out all convention.
Piggy karate-chopping the set to pieces, Kermit
crying on Elton John's sequined shoulder.
What was I at seven supposed to think about sex?

But what I wondered then about muppet
honey, I'm still fretting over as a man.
Those e-mails hawking porn aren't in
my box by *total* accident.

If it doesn't fit, I don't force it.
It's not intimacy, but for me it's working.
As a kid I was also confused by the cue
ball's ability to find its way to the return hole time after time.
I'd scratch and scratch just to bring it back
and now something inside me has been damaged.
Night rolls into sensual night and into night again.
Other men in love, or not, concentrate on baseball.
I don't blame my bachelorhood on only knowing
the shape my own weird love will make.
Hold me in your arms. Tune the channel to fire and flesh.

What the Sous Chef Knows

is the eventual Braille
brought on by cut onions—

the stick of garlic on skin,
and how its white husk leaves

the bulb like a sheath off her knife.
The combination to the meat locker,

and how much filet to clean on Wednesday
afternoons, that her line cooks are always right

no matter what the stiffshirts out front say. She knows
how starch in the air can taste like its giver, gold potato

releasing the black earth, pasta, broccoli stems—asparagus
snaps. How to make the most of the thinnest tuna loin.

She knows how to sew her own thumb closed—
which dishwasher to let go, which to take home.

Timeless dreams of slicing. Cold, solo sheets.
The sun on set, cooled outside her

blue cafe's back door screen, nothing
about it rare, or done well. How to

crack a white egg in each hand
and flick the lifeshell

down a stainless steel sink.

Flight Crew

Those who need to know
are always the last.
Foot odor—arrivals and departures, bad breath—
it's a shame the mind only gets the body
once a little time has passed:
Misaligned buttons. Spinach in teeth. Adultery.
Those who need to know
are always the last
call away from sober, one step from real disaster.

Take this new couple on their midnight rendezvous.
Their bodies are the one last purchase:
Luggage. Jet lag. Her toenail makes its mark
along his calf in the dead of night.
The need to come together half in lust, half defeat, puts
his head on a swivel.
And his heart has no true flight plan. Hers? No relief.
Those two lovers—anyone getting laid on stand-by
at baggage claim with a ticket for need, not wanting to be airborne last

in the flight their marrow takes into the heartloin—will they ever catch
that plane back to the mainland of no remorse, no regret?
It's a shame that Heart has no mayday, no point
of no return switch to turn off what we knew,
when we knew it, and when we knew we'd have to ditch.

Tilt-A-Whirl

. . . so this good friend of mine is looking for love,
 and she tells me one night her grandparents have called it quits.
"My grandmother says she's trading that bastard in
for some good magnets. She's been sewing linen pads full
of iron pellet bird shot into each
hip pocket, says it levels the red blood
cells in her hips. Says she'll just walk
anywhere she needs to go." We walked back to my place.
A cold mist forgave everything before us, and things coming up.

"Be home by eight, the earth's magnetic poles are switching tonight"
my ex-fiancé once asserted in a note, she, the physicist,
knew the apogee and circumspect of each astral body. "It's been 26,000 years,"
the note said, "and Vega is the north star once again."My books showed all the
points in different places,
but something beneath us shifted to her side of the planet.

I'm at a friend's house tonight, a couple gone to a weekend wedding.
I'm throwing biscuits to their dog-child. The storm of their lives, work, wine
and weekends
barely gives Zoe here her daily dose
of what passes for love.
My friends are good people. They've got a tornado
of black word magnets across their icebox:

This is a house to live and love in,
A man is no more than a woman,
and *Look at the size of that tool.*
It means nothing

stuck just below *Please, for God's sake,*
take out the trash and I imagine then my friends
coming to the kitchen at midnight
for a cool pear, or an innocent ice cube.

I'd like to scramble those words around
a bit, at least throw their verbs
down the sink. But in the gravity
of my latest hour, at midnight,
26,000 years could go by and my mind
would simply close around another foreign star
as alien and magnetic.
I can stick to any like metal. I'll kill to be close.

Emerge

Last night doing laundry I run
into the woman I could never forgive
myself for losing. Stopping for a late-night

snack, we try to make peace over a few beers
and fulfill an appetite that's safe.
We were never the sort who split things

down the middle, but tonight—me pepperoni,
hers exotica—cilantro and jerk
chicken—our eyes meet and something tells

us that's how it always really was, but hunger
kept us blinded, and thirsty for more.
Tonight it's just two diners at one table—

I see an absence of pigment—ring-shaped—
around her one finger. She sees me seeing
and says," Your hair has really gone gray."

The old competition, but we need it to be tame
this time, so we wade through a few kids
at the pool table to play a game: *Space Invaders*.

At each stage, those aliens eat more and more earth.
Our match ends. The pie comes hot, we eat
what we can, then share the rest like friends must.

After midnight, I'll slide through the kitchen in fresh socks—
the taint of Cheer and Joy still beneath my nails—
and chew a cold slice of last night, quiet

as my clean, solo sheets. Unfriendly as coins
blasted back from the fountain.

Working Out in the 21st Century

Staring at female breasts, *good ones*,
my trainer'd specified, is the same for a man
as thirty minutes of cardiovascular exercise.
I thought, It's a wonder I'm not in better shape—

but what about that *good ones* thing in there?
Who's to say what's this or that?
At the gym, shapes and spandexes,

the breasts all look pretty good to me.
Even in the breasts at which many men
would look down their noses

I seem able to find some goodness.
The breast is holy, and still, it's fine the soul
has no muscle tone, and relies on the human heartloin

to tell it what to flex. We're built
like this because it fits so nicely.
And the attraction is more than architecture

and exercise, it's loneliness desperate to hear
he now, finally, has a fighting chance at slimness.
But being that man, I wondered about the penis.

Will a woman experience the equivalent
of thirty minutes of cardiovascular exercise
if she stares at one good penis? More? Less?

And what makes a penis good? I bet at least half
of us, men and women, have something to say
about good penis qualities. Look.
Who really knows what to run after?

I'm not a person who needs to lose
a lot of pounds, and I could lap
these same solo miles anywhere—
Boston, Pittsburgh, Broken Bow—

then shower at home, and eat alone.
I'm not someone bent on building
a new, buff me. I'm working hard
each afternoon for my heart.

You Are Here

Each beginning is the furthest thing
from my mind. To be hot, and hell bent
on the beginning means I've borne an ending,

but come full circle just to wind
up back where I started. To circumvent
the beginning is the furthest thing

from the heart when you find
a new lover's hand on the back of your neck;
a beginning means to have stomached an ending.

None of us have loved and not been unkind.
We Braille through each other's lives and forget
why each beginning is the furthest thing

from the ending, which would give anything to be the beginning.
I know I've dragged my feet through love, only to regret
that sweet beginning. It means I've sweated out the end

of something now left behind, and reminds
my heart (and mind) why—even foolish, even still suspect—
each beginning blinds, and blinds again.
Who wouldn't want to start and see the end?

The Morning After

my body makes mistakes,
I don't blame bones; they'll set.
And they didn't mean to take

that tack—it was my heart
in hunger, anger, deceit.
When her body breaks

the rules of pattern; passion, blame,
our habit, new ground, rhythm, sweat—
I always seem to take

for granted the ruin once there. No pain
no gain in each human resource? Huh. I bet
when the first two bodies make

dumb love in the next universe, still homesick too,
they'll ache like us for the broken pieces left.
Trying to forget as best we can, there's no mistaking

beginnings for endings for good reasons.
Me? Hole-hearted? I promise to be good, lust, to regret
it when our bodies screw up, make those muscular mistakes.
If true love gives us the finger, that's the breaks.

To a Young Couple Planning Their First Vacation, Thinking of Divorce

If one of you drops a body towel
in the sea, and in packing after vacation
someone balls it up and stuffs it
in the trunk, it will still be wet
when you get home. You can almost taste salt

just touching the corners. When you pull
into the driveway shaking sand and sense
from you, from each other, and the front
door lock is unfriendly as the cold

sheets you'll share, stretch that towel across
the backyard fence. The neighbors will know
you're home, they'll see what hope two weeks has come

to bring you, in that towel, in its braided mold.
And when the thing dries—when the fabric
grows stiff and takes on shape of the wire teeth
in each wrought chain link—when last year's thistle
still blocks your shed, throw the towel away.

It's a mess, after all, it was never meant
to hold so much mineral. The bare
threads still left from all the days you've made
wouldn't even dry one dish, not one body.

New Transfer

Working All the Angles

At a conference last month a colleague
pointed out a striking couple to me,
a tall woman with wiry red hair, and thick glasses,

even at that distance I could tell they were thick,
and a round, pear-shaped man with a lot of hair.
"Those two are doing serious work

in the world of poetry these days."
I drained the last of my wine,
and slunk behind my friend with her glass too,

thinking that I'd swipe a good look as I passed
to fill our glasses with a Portuguese red called *Est*.
Yes, her glasses were thick, and skewed her face—

but his shape was more figgy than pear,
and I could now see the hair was false—
plus he had artichoke dip, just a dab

of it, on the very tip end of his nose.
I filled our glasses with *Est*, and like a human
chain of want, this figgish poet raised his brows

at me, and one-by-one'd to me the plastic cups of he
and this tall woman-poet, and asked
me "Would you be so good?"

I said I would, and did, and as the man

handed back his partner's wine,
just a trickle managed to scumble
down the front of her rose-cotton
blouse. He produced a handkerchief
from somewhere, daubed
it on her small breast, and she did not flinch, but
rather arched her back a bit toward him.

I thought then of the serious work going on
in their world, and what poems they were reading
to each other, whose toothbrush
was beside whose spit cup,

what flavor coffee they shared,
all the gossipy bits
I could then run and tell the rest of the talkers
who must've seen a glint

of what I'd sort of caused. She smiled
her thank you at him, and took the dab
of dip off his nose with her fingernail, the long nail

of her left pinky finger, then put that nail in her mouth.
Like a small, red bird, a second wing found
in the breaking and shedding of the first—

I remembered once hearing my parents making love, working
very hard to make it right while I sat listening
through thin heartwalls of my room,
serious work in the world of children.

Desiderata Redux

Dear editor:
Please accept the following poems for consideration in your upcoming issue.
My poetry has been seen in Gotta Right Network Litmag, and local newspapers
here in Polix, Arizona. I have been running my own paranormal investigations
business, drinking hard, reading ancient history and grieving continuously
since the unsolved disappearance of my wife, and best friend of eighteen years.
I believe this gives my work a distinctive spirit and makes these poems worth
publication in your periodical.

Dear editor:
Please accept the following poems for consideration in your upcoming issue,
my first book of poems, *Small Things*, was selected by The Lower Rhode Island
Poetry Society as fifth runner up in the Lower Rhode Island Poetry Society
Chapbook Contest. I am an Assistant Patient Care Assistant with the Lower
Rhode Island Hospice. My poems have also appeared in *Poetry Rhode Island*,
and *Rhode Poems*. I believe the worldliness of my verse makes these poems
worth publication in your periodical.

Dear editor:
Please accept the following poems for consideration in your upcoming issue. I
have been the recipient of two Goldfish Fellowships to study and translate
ancient Olmec poetry, and have been teaching poetry writing from the platform
of Plato's Republic for the US Naval Academy these last ten years. My poems
have appeared in *Tokyo Quarterly Haiku, Paradelles from Cannes, The Brunei
Ghazal* and *Poems That Might Have Come From God's Mouth*. My first four
books of poems now regularly appear in rotating shows for the MOMA and the
Guggenheim. I've been commissioned by the Vatican to create poetic frescoes
for the last ten Popes, have won the Nobel Prizes in Literature and Peace each
twice, and just last year took the silver medal for the 15,000m during the
Summer Olympics in Kenya. I believe these poems may be worth publication in
your periodical.

Observations During a Flat Tire Repair Across the Street From PS 39 Elementary, New York, NY

When I left the psychic reading
at your upper east side apartment,
I just knew something was wrong. The angle of light
setting west through each chocolate leaf
of Central Park washed my car in a slanted way.
Someone had slashed my left, rear Goodyear,
only one of the four as if to say,
"See how far that donut in the trunk gets you."

But a flat tire isn't something you can hate.
The damage is repairable. It's the chance to prove
to everyone you've got what it takes.
The first graders at recess from PS 39
watched me bring out the spare and jack
like apprentice surgeons in a theater, consulting
behind cupped hands as I rolled my sleeves back.

The kids were typical—urban Korean-American
Creole, South African, West Indian orthodox Catholics—
and began to act my misfortune out upon themselves
in a harmless parody only children could master:
One knelt as the car, on all fours, and more bent down
to slash his legs, to scream "Help, police!" to take down
each store's awnings, to sweep the walks
and ticket double-parkers and mug old ladies,
to sell hot dogs and pizza from white carts.
Two Jews pointed at a black boy and sneered "Nigger"
and he sneered back, "You're goddamn right,"
three girls held back a forth as she gave birth screaming
"Jesus—doctors—what was I thinking?"
I remembered then what the psychic had said

to you, our hands clasped above the black rocks
and chicken bones you'd thrown down: "I know a great
dermatologist—remind me to give her name
and number to you." The pregnant girl jumped up and paid
the doctors for their service, her fingers
pressed make-believe money in their palms.
It looked like tiny cities being built in their hands.

Bohemian Landscape

Good Humor bells are ringing.
It's America in summer.
Freezers are full of sweets.

But we haven't yet left
our soaked footprints in concrete.
I still want to swim between your legs,

rising just in time to shout *Polo!*
and understand at last the human current
sweeping all of us from treading water

into what our parents will always hope and fear for us,
a smooth ride up the untopable wave of life.
I'm dragging in a sofa from the shed
wrapped in plastic still. And there's always
a shovel caked in black dirt leaned against the parlor wall.

My own mid-life dreams leave me
breathless as losing virginity.

Nothing stays the same as it ever was.
If we could go back, we'd just look back from there
and wish we didn't know some silent floor
awaits us at the blue deep end.

It's a prayer far beyond even our incredible makers'

best intentions. So we soak in it
and breaststroke until we prune.

Metropolitan Heart

I am never coming back to New York City.
The Yankees have lost. The Knicks have lost. The Mets
have lost, Tito Puente has died, and the service
in Spanish Harlem is being held during the worst rainstorm
anyone can remember. There's not a dry face in town.

The ticker at 5th and Wall street has stopped.
The whores, pimps, pushers and addicts have
all started Internet enterprises, are selling different options
from the shadows. They're hooked in like never before.
Coney Island is deserted, Nathan's has no brauts,

The Cyclone has finally fallen—finally.
Radio City has canceled each 7:55 show.
At Thomas and Cooncoe's, someone has stolen the eight ball
from table thirty-seven, and not
one straight cue is free.

On Tuesday, I heard Luna's in Little Italy served
their first bad mussel ever, and today, Charlie's
in The Silk Ghetto is full of Wops, Kikes, Spics,
Niggers, Towelheads, Rickies, Queers, Micks,
WASPs and Frogs, they're waiting in line
out the door, but there's not one Chink in the place.
Every slice of pizza from each white street cart
at all the city's gridlocked intersections has turned grey.
Each vendor there is neatly shaved.

No one's pissing in the gutter.
The Rangers have lost, the Islanders have lost. The Mets
have lost, Tito Puente has died. The service
in Spanish Harlem is being held
during the worst rainstorm anyone can remember.

But I'm the wax angel cast down
into asphalt hell, and I can hear my own
metropolitan heart melting, whisper up
from the subways and heat grates—it's just a murmur:
"Make truth," I think I hear,
or "grapefruit," I can't be sure.
The sun moves west like always.

In the Salon of the Centro Artistico, 1933

... from the crepuscule of the ring, Lagartijo with his Roman duende,
Joselito with his Jewish duende ...
  —F.Lorca

The cantaor is drum and devil.
This is it—things are beginning
to happen, everyone has moved inside.

Direction is coming (like the soul's dark wing
which knows all color) with everything
the crowd has come to expect

from that black moment of horrible dance
each soul begs to take with them when they leave.
German and Portuguese thick the air, people

are calling for more wine, that new cask of *Est*
from Lisboa, but the waiters speak to no one,
nod to one another from across the room, and

not a drop is touched. The kerosene lamps
have been turned as high as they'll go
without smoking, their wide light climbs

the stucco walls. The cantaor is drum
and devil, a hungry ghost, things are beginning to happen.
Everyone has given up

on more wine and has settled like a salon
crowd will when it's time, everyone, it's time,

it's time. Outside
across the lop-eared square, in the tight blue
café shadows that keep light in its natural places,
the fiery local women have stopped dancing

for just a moment. Their blue-black hair
sticks wet to their faces. Because it's Sunday
and the *futball* games have finished,

the younger *Benefica* players
are with these dancing local women.

They've won today, and know they're welcome
in the salon, but stay instead
with the local dark-skinned women.

The light outside crawls down
the worn stucco walls. *Benefica*
players look at the world

around them like old, uncle dogs,
an absence of light means
nothing to them, they can hear

the cantaor from where they are
in the quiet, blue café shadows
outside across the lop-eared square with the wild local women—

and they're full with wine, that new cask of *Est* from Lisboa.

Red and Return

Jolek, young, and stupid, did not die
in the Nazi death camps. Instead, he cut
off his own left hand around January 19
40, at Birkenau, or Sosnowiec. Three feet
from an infirmary, or a cafeteria,
with a hatchet, across an Oak tree stump
or a make-shift plyboard bench like an overgrown
root come due, Jolek cut off his own left hand.
True, he was still right-handed—with that good
right hand Jolek banged through the clinic (mess hall) doors,
"My hand, my hand!" he cried, and they starched
the wound closed, but no one would touch
Jolek's lost left hand back out in the cold.
The Polish kapo who'd seen the whole thing
forbade anyone to go near it, the story goes, and in hopes

of buttering up told the sergeant
(after losing in cards the night before), who told
his captain, who thought the story unusual,
a Jew cutting off his own left hand. This captain
went first to Jolek in the infirmary and asked,
 "Why? Why would you cut off your own left hand?"
but Jolek had no answer, would not tell why,
and the captain was so taken by the (lack of) story
that once Jolek's arm had "healed" he was given
the kapo position over ninety-five older prisoners,
and Jolek beat them with his good right hand,
beat them as he clutched his stump to his chest,
and made them jump and dance til they passed out.

                    But before all this,
as that captain left the infirmary he stopped
to stoop at the still-bleeding, still-shivering left hand,
"Look," he gestured to the sergeant—actually a friend
from Dachau, or Wiesloch, from before the war—
there in the web of Jolek's left thumb and forefinger,
in prison ink blue, was a dime-sized tatoo
of the Star of David, lots of Jews had them—
in different body places—and as they looked,

in January's cold fist, the story goes, Jolek's hand
turned blue and the tattoo disappeared.

It was an amazing thing to watch, I imagine,
and that captain and the sergeant talked about it
over the years and stayed friends, and thought a lot
about being called upon to do something bad—

called upon by your country to do something
bad, because they were not animals, or demons,
but workaday men and not sure about that even, I found out:
I met them both on the way to Dachau, by coincidence,
absolute luck at a tram stop near the Munich airport (moving through
after a funeral for the one's brother, or wife) and we just struck
up a chat, in English, and talked about the war
because I asked. Compelled, I think, by Jolek's hand, by memory,
like breaking open, they cut each other off
telling me how this Jewish man named Jolek
chopped off his own left hand with a hatchet, Jolek
who wouldn't take the hand back, Jolek with his left arm
clutched to his chest the rest of the year—how
they'd watched the Jew in Jolek disappear from his body.

Jolek, Jolek, Jolek, until I just had to tell them—
had to tell them about my Great-Uncle Jolek,
young and mean and stupid, who did not die
in the Nazi death camps but rather cut off his own left hand
and that no one in our family ever knew why, and it's true,
it's true, I said I wouldn't lie to you, sir, and we
sat quiet for a moment. We embraced then, I hugged
him hard like I would my good father, and he hugged back hard,
I don't know why, but it's how my story goes.
In his eyeglasses lay everything cracked—forgiveness, pride
and clean anger—or maybe it was my reflection in those lenses,
but I knew then that losing a hand, even cutting
off another man's hand means only half
what it takes to cross the human heart.

Roast

In this valley, sweet smoke. From the black
cooker at the edge of their lot, my fiancée's
father leans in: "It's late August. The pigs
are just right for picking."

When the sun drops down
over blue bowls of black
walnuts and sound begins to travel in the cooler air
my life comes clear as the jelly in Gefilte fish jars:
"What's she marrying that kike for anyway?"

Three young sons of so-and-so have found

a turtle, and with a bit of neck bone, are coaxing it toward the grease drip.
I'm at the end of the line. I take some brown beans, and cover them with slaw.
In a week I'll be hungry, dipping apples in honey.

An Apple from Dachau

It's the eighteenth day of Nissan,
the first month of the Jewish year, April 21st—
Passover's third day. I'm on a backways cobblestone street.
"Liebling," a woman selling apples says to me
but I don't speak German. She smiles, and nods
to the euro coins in my palm.

It's one fine apple, shining up at me
from the center of my hand. And still
I have no idea how to be sacred.

Any fruit, even just the core
or shed skin, is holy when you're lonely.

At dusk, with a cup of rum-laced tea, I watch
out my window to where the vendors stay out at their carts
until the light goes dead, eating Whitefish
from wax paper, and one half of an orange.

Something so beautiful as to give up seed
is lonely, and to shed its skin for hunger is holy.
If you plant an apple seed in the far town field
where snow never stays, even in winter,
and that seed lives, it's a holy, holy thing.

Not like Gefilte fish. Right now
thirteen hours east, my mother
is in Brooklyn buying two pounds
of Whitefish, Carp and Pike flesh,
chances are the fishmonger
knows her: You'll never find bones,
it's why my relatives always have
Passover at my parent's house.
Keep the shed skin, my mother will tell the Fishmonger
but she's keeping the head, seed and core. The first
spring I remember smelling those fresh
fish bones, I was five. It was the salt smell
fleshwork of my young hunger. My mother will grind
the fish together with seltzer water, nutmeg,
white wine and finely diced celery ribs
while thinking about something sacred.

Anything so beautiful as to give up its hunger
for holiness, and shed its skin for the sacred childheart
is still not enough, won't show me how to love. And there's nothing
edible in this poem. Nothing holy.
Only an apple, which tastes like apple, smells
like an apple. What else can an
apple mean here, in any other holy place it's the same, sweet fruit—
but on this cobblestone street
in Dachau where my grandmother
is said to have been beaten to death
and no one said Kaddish until a few minutes ago, I would eat
six million perfect apples as the one here in my palm and never feel full.
I'd embrace hundreds of loving and hating
Germans, Koreans, Catholics, Laotians, real women
and men, anything to let go of the ancient shadowboxer
in me who snorts *nation*
with each jab and wide hook—the one
seed who's never known an enemy
besides his own, dark imagination.

I can't start my life over. The landmarks
I know are all in poems, not in people's hearts.
There are no clear landmarks in this poem.
When I cross back over the Atlantic to Troy,
New York—home—her milling ball quarry machines
and cookie factories burned like figures
my own youth had no time for—inside the American
womb of plenty up above our sacred, holy world
I'll eat this apple, I'll split it with
my mother and sisters over Halvah, macaroons.

Family Business

Take All the Time

Put the T-shirt in the window
and hit the hazards. Blame it all
on the price of gasoline, but have faith.
On the next earth, even the dead
get one lift back into town.
It's why I'd swear I've seen

my father again. On line
at Schrop's Bakery, or he's holding a sparkler
for the Fourth of July.
He hands the spitting firework to a bratty child.
It's not me. The kid's got one of those
blonde mullet-mohawks, and his arms are crossed.
I know it takes more than loss, and a bit
of bad vision to get to grace. Needle on 'E'
sooner or later, everyone leaves

but if one of us, so long ago, could give
each known star a name and story
I pray we're not too far from losing
the desire to see where being goes.
Left sock stuck halfway down my tank, one heel
of the loaf left, only a swallow of booze—
I have faith anyway. Those constellations
furthest from us feel just fine from here.

Camera Obscura

God works in mysterious ways—*not!*
Idiot lights. CAUTION—HOT. WILL CAUSE

SEVERE TIRE DAMAGE. The chance to prove you've got
what it takes is so often fraught with odd challenges:

Denver Soufflé. LIGHT FUSE—GET AWAY.
That prophylactic pause at any altitude, under

any time delay. God works in mysterious ways
and not one person doesn't still wonder

what the hell they've done. Warts. Bad teeth. Spot
on your wife's left lung, the heartbreak of

psoriasis. The wish bone always breaks—what God saw in the mirror,
stripped naked, waiting for the kiln to get too hot?

Who knew that clay would be so brittle, so sweet,
we'd forget, reach out and touch that hot plate twice but

never blame the body until blood and feces finally come
together in the terrible dark. God works in mysterious ways

and not for gain or gift. Huh-un. I hate mysteries. I jump at
cliffs instead of clinging. At my end, give me grit:

a simple, ruined western, good in black, bad
in white. The sun doing just what it knows it should.

Getting It Again

As a kid I got oral sex
all wrong: I heard the expression
and pictured the happy couple
sitting up in bed fully clothed,
literally discussing the specifics
of what would soon take place.

Now a little older, I'm happy.
I've gone down that road and figured
things out: Making sexual love—
working hard to make it right—
takes a brand of brain that goes
beyond the simple knowing of what

goes where, that one act's certain
structure takes practice. Finding partners
has always been a chore I'm just
not up to: I can't dance, the toilet seat is always up—
there's a burned out bulb in my fridge.
Rather than beginnings and endings
I guess I'm more of a blow me a kiss
from a distance kind of guy.
Don't get me wrong—it's not you, and it's
not the *it's not you it's me* thing—but tonight, half-gone

in that darker sleep, if my big toe's nail
puts its mark along your calf, forgive me.
Take these words from my mouth.
Replace them with your name.

My Father Teaches Me What it Means To Burn

When I was twelve a cinder singed my eye,
fused beneath the lid past tweezers' reach
and drained the tender color from my sight.

My father had torched the aging oak that summer night.
Struck by the blaze—beyond speech
when I was twelve—a cinder singed my eye.

I shrank as the gray branches died,
melting down to pupil black, to dark bleach
the tortured color from my sight,

bleeding gasoline, rising through flames of height.
My tree hushed down to ashes. I wept.
When I was twelve, ocean-eyed and thin,

this tree had been a green climb
from home to hope, familiar bark and seamless sleep.
Now, the color faded from my sight,

my father tells the tale with wry pride:
"Burning trees feeds the soil," he'd preach then too,
when I was twelve, a cinder in my eye.
I'd give anything to trade that fire for light.

The Problem with Crumbs

Sisters get hungry.

The sylvan floor is damp.

A hint of yeast attracts insects.

Birds can see even seeds from great heights.

Gingerbread smells so good in the wrong forest,

that smell can make your brother forget his own careful pattern—

might make your parents throw you out like day-old bread.

Swine Logic

In the time of pigs and wolves
and the regularity of speaking

creatures wrought with instinct
and the taste for blood,

I'd have thought like pigs;
I, too, would've believed in the progression

of what seemed safe. When all you've ever known
are fields of mud, some black straw laced

straight and patched with your own shit seems
like it will hold you and your siblings tight—

then some bad ass blows the whole deal down.
So you go to wrist-thick sticks—same deal—then bricks;

A thumb print over your x-rayed heart.
Feeling the phone might ring, or go quiet forever.

A story with its lesson in metastasis,
death in a wolf's baptismal breath: huff, huff, huff.

The world outside begins its howl of hope against you.
You play sincere Pinochle with kin in candle-shadows, confident . . .

Tennis Lessons

At twelve, my sensitive uncle

gave me *Leaves of Grass*. At thirteen, his sister

my mother—drunk on Orange Blossoms, orange juice

and gin—snatched the book from me after I'd ignored her latest

dumb mumblings, and curled it up in the Cuisinart chute, long, long lines

collecting in the Lucite bin. I saved those verses, and have kept them

in a bronze pill bottle on whose red longitudinal label—with one

eye in deep swoon—it is written, *Warning—Do Not Take*

On An Empty Stomach. May Cause Blurred Vision. Will

Discolor the Urine. Affects Breathing. Only For Internal

Use—Keep Out of Reach of Children.

When I Need a Moment

It's not often I think of my parents
while masturbating. I hope that doesn't surprise you.
But lately my father has been slipping into my fantasies.

It's truly bizarre. There I'll be, happily
inside that made prism—Chevy back seat,
cool silk sheets at The Plaza, whatever—

when from that perfect room's most perfect chair,
or turned around, arm over the headrest, my dad will say
"How's it going back there?" or "I'll be in the head

if you need me." With fierce passion and desperate
impatience I push him away in my mind I tell him
to fuck off, like I did April of '79 on Lime Street:

He'd been teaching me to drive a standard shift.
My hand jerking the stick to all points of the compass,
clutch burning sickly sweet—I even knew then it would take

all I would ever have to just match the random
gracelessness of my silly little life. We've all been caught
with our hands down our pants by figures who created us with clean lust.

I won't let it bring me down. If my brain screws up
and mistakes love for love that's fine—it's good, it's enough.

Old Bird

Every mother ingests
something no one else will stomach.
It's true, you know:

a swallow was
actually eaten to catch the daddy
long-legs which crawled

down her esophagus
after the drosophila, all done for me.
I would never know hunger.

It happened at dawn.
I was the kitchen son, hiding in the pantry.
Cracking open another cold can,

the specter
of Pierre Cardin and Lilac Vegital
still hanging around,

my old lady
swallowed each creature whole—
fang, feather, wing.

Over the longest distances
I have blamed my bones for needing
A different way to be touched.

Ashes over water,
I will never make peace
with my myths:

There's a spider in the salad
nicoise, Oleander berries scraped over bread.
I spread my own black feathers

and pick at the dead.

Goose

I'd been telling girls the scar
came from rock, paper or scissors, that

no one in my family can remember
who said what and when, or why.

I was an only child, and my parents
can agree about challenges, the hands

across the dinner table and the one, two *three—* !
But causation? I say an old game turned sour.

My father swears inattention to the rules.
My mother circles our table with her biscuits, layer upon flake

which she sets on each plate, *duck, duck, duck* . . .

Progression

"This report is designed to show you the progress your child is making. We would like to call your attention to the fact that no two individuals are alike in all respects. Please do not, therefore, compare your child with other children, but measure him according to his own ability."
—Margaret Mayberry, Teacher, Royal Oak Day School

Jesse has good potential. He plays with a variety of items from the shelf
each day, and usually chooses those which can best be enjoyed when shared
by one or more children. At snack time
Jesse is always the first to share
his desire for another student's cookies.
Jesse is capable of following directions when given
to the group as a whole, but often fails to then use the proper
procedure necessary to crown an assignment correctly, or in a timely fashion.
Jesse needs to improve his ability

to control his emotions; he is happy when he is the leader of the project
but if another child wants to change the pattern or move to another activity
Jesse exhibits his frustration by crying, sulking, or striking out physically.
Jesse's primary mode of communication is verbal.
Jesse's speech is fluent and articulate. When he vents
anger or frustration, the tone of his voice changes.
His voice becomes extremely loud and high-pitched.
Jesse has problems discerning certain shapes against others,
lowercase 'b' and lowercase 'd,' circles and spheres, squares against rectangles.
Jesse gets himself ready for dismissal, and only needs help snapping his coat.
Jesse knows the basic colors.
Jesse is showing daily improvements in his ability to cut with scissors.

Jesse is not the kid who ran away with the circus, is not
on the highwire hung over no net. Jesse doesn't defy death.
Jesse's car pulls a little to the left, and the rear tires
leak. He has flat feet, and his dog has cancer.
Half the world laughs, half the world cries.
Jesse's front door lock echoes in the empty foyer
when I click it awake. And there waiting for me in the hallway
mirror, is a child chasing every word he knows.

Reading "The Three Billy Goats Gruff" to My Son on the One-Year Anniversary of My Divorce

The second goat
knew just enough:
how to be bigger

than the first
and to set a stage
for his brother's
gruesome act.

Poor, poor troll (poor me)—
only child of the bridge-grave—
get off the road, forgive us.
Don't breathe
a word of this to anyone.

Prayer for an Elegy

Rock doesn't mind what we've named it.
Fire seems fine with our label. Water
could care less if words
get it right or not.

I am making no preparations
for the next world.
If our lexicon for this earth
can't get me closer than this

stone me. Burn me. Drown me.
Stop the slow heart knocking.
Tell me all about loneliness in the dead
of night, and tell it to me soon.

Over Time

Gathering the Last Young Day

1. Dawn

Heatless light spills out onto hundreds of *The Norfolk Times*
scattered around my feet in front of the Be-Lo Market in Cape Joseph,
the town where I first fucked and fought, a town in a coma:
One floor schoolhouse in 1983. 216 students K through 12,
The Chesapeake in two directions, the Atlantic in the other.
One restaurant, Etz's, where one pound
of steamed crabmeat, just picked, with corn
off the cob directly, in 1983, $4.99.

I want to describe to you the picture
I've been seeing in my dreams, a scene
that comes at morning, and is morning,
the same morning as the last 153 days
of my childhood. I delivered newspapers.
I was fifteen. At morning, before dawn,
the smells of creosote and tar
from the coal and ice plant across Peppermint Street
would bleed their new daily creations
into the town's wind.
There's no sound, and I ache
with something I remember not knowing about yet . . .

Those toxic smells, they are then in 19
83 just newer to me than my
split newspaper bundles. The Be-Lo behind me offers
nothing: neat bins of vegetables, and bottles
of Mr. Clean, his face smiling down, the shine of cold morning
that crawled up the concrete grime and red rust bloom
of each grocery cart lined outside, all make the sun
a twisted, heatless winter star.
I'm slipping my newsie gloves

over the fingers of hands I thought I'd lost,
but they have slid back and gathered their soft shapes.

2. Noon

Alarm clock, sun and shaving, a white absence of pigment
still missing in a ring-shape where my ring finger
meets my hand. The day's first cigarette.

My own coffee and oranges.
My own two salami lunch sandwiches on peasant bread
wrapped in wax paper.
                              Yesterday I wristed away a third leather
watch band, and lost a third timepiece in the deep salt and sun of the six to six
        shift
putting down the seed of life at Bronson's Aqua-Farm.
I watched it sink like a newly minted
quarter into the murk of the Chesapeake.
Clams get planted like children in a classroom,
classrooms in a one-room school: Under mesh net and tiny gravel
like grey baby teeth, the little seeds rest in long plastic trays
that will stick to the palms like wool if your hands are dry.
One man and me hip-float these trays through thigh-deep water,
Virginia sun and cigarette ash—vicious, red jellyfish
we call Lion's Manes for their thick, red tentacles.
Then we feel with our feet
where the last tray's track rests
in proportion to the rest, and squat to set the children
in crab-thick sand for the coming year.
Only the mesh net protects the seed from life.
Soon the trays plot out, eight by five, forty trays
to a school. On a cold morning like this, I can stand on top
of the sea oat dune above that inlet with the day's second cigarette
and see our plots stretch back into the horizon.
                              But right now, in this sunlight,
there's a half cup left, and the front page of *The Norfolk Times* reads:
We Turn 50 Today. I remember watching them turn thirty-five too,
at fifteen, delivering newspapers under a January sun coming in
through a wound opened over Cape Joseph by the east wind's cold knives . . .

The sun now at 6 AM seems to be rising,
but it's so cold out it could be setting.
The difference is discernable
as the gray lines on each print page.
I reach for my coffee and crab gloves, and wonder
for the umpteenth time if I'll taste
tomorrow's supper again in the burned sides
of tonight's coffee. The clamming weather, the winter water
with its crab claw mornings and the occasional black ray,
has burned its loneliness into me deep this year—
I can feel it hiss each day
like a curse at the heart of my bones.
But the heart that beats blood into those bone-hearts

has always been a rotten thing—now, but then too, at fifteen:

Each Wednesday morning I'd raid the pastry cart
some poor baker would leave for the Be-Lo
just minutes before I'd arrive—either back
from a run to fill my basket with papers, or a little late,
just getting started. I'd wait, hiding
behind the ice and coal plant with my bike, or around
this one dead sycamore that still, today, hasn't dropped.
He had thin, blond hair, a round
kind face and wire glasses, and cheap brown shoes.
I remember his green truck with double back doors . . .
I never said a single word to him.
I never waived to him.

He'd putt-putt-putt away, and I'd gorge
down sumptuous breakfasts of raspberry tart
smeared with newsprint, still-warm lemon pie soaked
in the stench of stretched rubber bands.
I never said a single word.

3. *Dusk*

I was too young to know what work is,
but not too young to know that I didn't yet want to know
what it means to truly work—to struggle
with the hard labor of the lonely
morning workers of the world, the bakers, the fishermen,
the farmer and the mother, and the father.
But it's funny. Even then I knew
the world would sweep me bare, I knew I'd wear
these laceless brown work boots.

4. *Dark*

I'm not yet ready for my daily dose of ankle-deep
clam sand packed with a miniature version
of my every nightmare creature, Lion's Mane's burns,
Virginia winter light and cigarette ash—

even these newspapers really, Jesus I was bad:
                              In a spot
across the scum of trees which still separates
Cape Joseph, the Atlantic Ocean, and the Chesapeake Bay,

in a dug out root ball pit trenched in low
under the town's bulkhead I hid
those papers like booty. They wouldn't be delivered
for weeks it seems now, for months. No one knew the news and it was all my
        fault.
I hid the Tuesday election edition. The Thanksgiving circular.
It seems now that root ball pit was long black miles
wide, with no end, and could have held
a ticker-tape parade worth of print if I'd needed it to.

When I turn sixteen—on my sixtieth birthday—
in my greatest dreams the smell of pastry baking
will again wake Cape Joseph under the dead sycamore
at the end of my mind: The kindergarten teacher I bit,
Cindy Harris—Martin Syzna, the friend who swallowed mercury
and died so young, first gone blind—Gloria Tern, the first girl I hated,
and loved—my ex wife—my father . . .
They've all come to the Be-Lo in the fog of my old sorrow.
One by one they ask me for forgiveness,
I can hear them, and I reach out begging to be forgiven
but I cannot see one clear face—I see that I don't
know them anymore. Have I forgotten them?
Did they forget me? I'd give anything
to kiss them each one last time, on the cheek,
see my own eyes in theirs.

Their soft bodies burn away

in the light over the east wing roof

of the ice and coal plant across the street,

and there's a faceless boy in the Pittsburgh
of my last, young day, in Madison, in DeMoines, everywhere
I've ever been, or would've been, pedaling fast
in the cold morning's fist through block
on block of wet, lightless Annapolis street.
He's racing fast with a basket of the good news,
trying to beat that cold January rise,
and the world around him
moves like a scene in which
the day never gets past dawn's first rays.

A New Walk

for A.R. Ammons

Albert Goldbarth asked me to name a great poet
on the Wednesday before you died,
and I forgot you and said, "John Milton."

It's true, I'd loved Milton
longer than you, and given the island
and one book only, well . . .

Your death could not be simple for me
like Milton's, imagined and dry
as gold-leafed pages in leather:

It was cancer. It took life
while I was watching something else:
Those wild yellow daises, honeysuckle bushlimbs,

fluvio-glacial deposits, scattered cedarcone
I could only see, and not smell:
Fine, brown seedlings ground to grist,

the silent offering of your death.
But it isn't time to let things be,
to let the draft-books fall—

the song's improvident center
in me, still in you, still assures
the self that is ours, all of ours:

a new walk is a new walk.

Shoulder

The dog shakes you awake
in the dead of night—
needing water and love

too late, your child calls out—
What do you say?

So many nails on the freeway of the heart, and no AAA.

Cat hair all over the passenger's
seat; drive-thru by candlelite, and it's wrong and cold.
Pocketbook empty but a heart of gold—
you don't, but agree to say you did.
What a thing to say.

Gravel beneath your nail, white T-shirt
in the window, spot
on your sister's lung . . .
what do you say

if your mother finds
her husband's shattered heart
and can't make heads or tails
of the last forty-five years,

when the father-bucket drops down
and that well just echoes back dry
what the hell are you supposed to say?

I say, "Lean on me. It's okay.
Let's go, here's a real drink."
I say "I'll bury them the best I can,"

and I say nothing. Half-asleep, half-woken, the face

beside us at rest in its
comfortable indifference, it may
not even matter what gets said:

The dog goes out, but doesn't go—
kids get drunk on love
and have their hangovers.

Whoever gets it right? Who
knows what you're supposed to say,
and how to speak those words?

I have never really known what to say,

what I meant, or how to say it right.
But there's an all-nite diner on Front

and Market by the river. From where we are,
the sun moves west and always will.
Another bed awaits our ruins, then another

and another. The right things to
love – our thirsts, our hungers—over a cup
of black coffee and a warm Danish

we, the soulvoice, can maybe talk it all through.
Look around you. The light, the dark,
the check's on me.
What do you say?

Try This at Home

A cigarette happens just at the moment after.
The connections between sex and death let our lovers know we'd go

up in smoke when the moment is right. But take the black widows.
No shared luxury for them. Even if he does it just right, she bites his head off.
"It's for our kids" she says with her mouth full. No wonder no one
does it spider-style. Mexican Tree Slugs also have it tough. Once
joined, the friction of their sexual forces builds to an explosion that tears
their frail bodies to pieces which later feed their larval pods.
It's rewarding to imagine that what we make in love is the food
for what we make in love, and not just fuel for one kind of danger.
Like the fifteen year old in Vaijapur who, after her uncles
see her smoking in public, rape her, and force a hive a bees
into her throat. Such concern for each other must be borne by blood
and fire. There must be a heart somewhere in the body.

But where? Why does it sometimes avoid even the best of us?
It's the trail of smoke that told the Timucua and Inca
of the crucial difference between friend and foe.
Well, we know what became of them. They smoked chocolate wrapped in
gum tree leaves, and believed that owls singing brought terrible omens.
That fire popping, and spitting too much smoke, was a sign of war. Maybe their
    last.
Given the right conditions, even the tiniest sign becomes a sign for something
    else.

It's as if everything in our lives is governed by experts. 4 out of 5 doctors.

And the experts say we should work our hearts in the morning. That's when
energy is the highest. It's the same with love. Fall for him or her
at dawn. Make your bodies work as early as possible, because the days
get so long, even the box jellyfish, in their own darknesses, start
swimming toward the bottom when the surface becomes too hot for them.
But as even the most poisonous creatures on earth
they're willing to touch when necessary. How careful and deadly we are
with our bodies, and with the bodies of those we care for. My dog likes for me to
    stick
my pinky fingers in her ears and rub them raw, even if it means she'll cry
out in pain, she's back again, rubbing her head against my hand.

What should I do—deny her desire? "Little Mina," I say, "I don't want to poke
your brain. I don't want to kill you accidentally."

Because I will have to kill her one day, when I think

she's had enough, and the sky outside takes the pearl-gray of rain and makes it
sacred, something more holy than a suggestion of night.

They'll tell me to put her down. I like to think I'll raise her up

into that dark air. It's the kindest thing I can do for her when the moment is
      right.

In the sweet cadence of our dreams, I've reached out for you hoping only
you'd just reach back this time. But you spoke from that dream
and told me if I bought just one suit, you'd give me two more free.
Would you? It seems like such a great deal
on the surface, but there's always a condition when it comes
down to the specifics. As we get older, we rise a little earlier each day until we're
      eating
dinner at four in the afternoon. Life always finds its own way—this morning
I heard they'd found tiny beetles in baby formula.
Gay men and women can now adopt. And why
shouldn't they? How much would you pay for a grande latte?
How long would you take
to decide which child to save?
What if I wanted three suits for that one? What about thirty?
The soul is always looking for the best bargain, and wants to be frugal.

I have risen too early, and waited for the papers while upstairs, still rising to the
      light
we both thought would keep us young, luck and lust break over the horizon.
So let me get this straight. The small becomes the large if you rub it the right
way with the best power. The sweetest second can bleed into an hour,
and the tortured seconds burn back again toward the horrible people
we are in one hot moment.
Not this moment, though, when the trigger pulls itself, explodes
inside us both at once, and we call it coming. I'd stick fire in my mouth
for you, is what we must be saying. I'd bite my own head off and call it love.

Human Relations

I am the wound, I am the blade—

I am the making and the made—

I am the skin, and blood in bone—

I am December, I am June—

I am Jimmy Best, I am Samantha Worst—

I am the last and the first—

I am where storms begin—

I am crossed wood, and sin—

I am the crow at noon, dusk and dark—

I am the spear, I am the mark—

I am sound and I am wave—

I am the night, and the living, neon day—

I am pressure in this pregnant world—

Sunday Afternoon

Silence on the linoleum and the accuracy
of an electric guitar: The delivery services have made
their early rounds, and the sun has too. Yesterday's
paper sits beneath today's just left. A song I know
comes on the radio, but rather than sing along
I only mouth the words. That's easier to forgive.

By the bay windows an early Martin here in January sings
her vibrancy through this season hoping for the next,
and I with muffin and Yoo-Hoo, no fruit, watch
her sing and pretend she sings to me. It's like that
living alone, and being wary of what breaks open
in the afternoons – the eye that notices such a small bird
before anything else and tries to make something of it,
regularity of a little meal just to keep on living regular—
a broken heart out for a walk in the mind that keeps
on living and living.
                    It's this neighborhood of dread
that keeps me moving down to the corner store
for another lighter, another bar of cheap, brown chocolate.
Order keeps to itself, and you have to say that Death
is the mother of beauty because to think otherwise
feels unthinkable, and perhaps sinful. But the Martin isn't concerned
with sin. Regardless of season, or my mind or heart

after each dusk walk, what I can say in retrospection
or foresight won't measure up against the weight of knowing
what lies in waiting each afternoon for something to shift
and break the present cadence of footsteps.
But that's the way those things go, and sometimes
you can't know until afterwards: Columns of doubt
built trying to place events in line. Broken afternoons
that wait dog-like for me to stir. A—significance—before the big town
hill moves underneath and breaks my heart just in the soil's
smells, and its particular feel in my hands that still have
the bull-headedness to pull it up and smell it: Confidence but not convinced,
not real courage. Fear at its place in my life, but me
unable to figure this life from as objective a place
as I can manage – memories of more poignant walks on streets where faces
knew mine and didn't look back indifferently, no matter what looks
familiar, and what looks wrong, wrong.
To imagine fear without letting myself

fill over feels false, unthinkable to me.

                                 I've asked
myself, day by day, "Am I living through
an hour with nothing left worth giving
over but a second chance to repeat my first disasters?"
On wings that can't know what it means to sing
when singing needs doing, wings with voices
afraid to let loose, everything is racing toward
another version, issued out from the mouth
like a cloud breaking open full of rocks and dark salt.

Thirteen Motorcycles

I.

It's busy for Wednesday—Cooncoe's
in uptown Allegheny, Hump Day, I'm thinking—
over a third draught and the young couple in the back booth breaking up
I think of a postcard arrived today from Broken Bow,
Nebraska, my old address blacked away
with postmark ink.

Screwdrivers are always Cooncoe's Wednesday special.
She in that back booth raises her empty glass
to our barman, who nods back; her beau
twists his napkin into tiny shreds.
She's a cute brunette with a great mouth—
says something about his leaving on Friday.
I can't help cringing over their Thursday hours.

II.

Throw a broken dart in any direction
and you'll hit a poem about Pittsburgh.
There are millions of lonely lovers in lots of bars
tucked away safe in their separate booths,
the sound of east coast river water means
something different to each of them, or nothing,
until its absence leaves their flow tides barren.
For me the Iron City, the Pirates, the Steelers,
the Penguins even, so much black and gold, steel—
represent the place a mind can go and forge a heart.
But so is Boston, and Las Playas, Broken Bow . . .

III.

So that hand raises her glass toward the barman, and the half-moon
there in lipstick rises through the room
like one half-heart through smoke—
her young beau trails his finger across
the wet glass top of their empty table, lights
matches impatiently, lets them burn
until he can't hold them.
"You sound like every other 'grass
is always greener' son of a bitch

I ever laid eyes on," and he looks
at me through the barback mirror, so I give
him the best look I can: Better be sure, friend.

IV.

The road home stays brown any season, even at the riverbanks.
On my first two nights along the Cape Fear, looking for something
to drown my shyness, I watched the same three men run trot lines
down a dock length into the ginger-colored water
below—A chicken neck for every foot of line.
The third night I dreamt of that long, dark river
water, of possibility, saw my index finger tied to a line
of strange bodies all reaching back to the light
with that one tied finger, sinking still to the silent bottom
where not even the Port City's barge sounds at dawn can be heard.
In that dream, then and when I still have it, I'm willing
to sell each future dream to take it all back, to give everything
back and make at least one broken thing in my life
somehow last. On the fourth night I asked that river,
"Where are you taking me?" It could have been any river.
Any east coast river flowing back and back and wide.
You can't really start life over in another town.
The old life lingers, and it's hard to deny exactly what happened.
What makes us rests in different fogs, town to town,
ghost bodies making love the best we can?

I've been in town two months now.
I've been in town eight long years, and

after so many weary, last beers in cities
and bars like long-necked birds of solitude
with their beaks in armpit tucks,
I've found a cocktail glass just almost empty
sits on most bars the same way, single or double,
and the beautiful hand which holds it
always wants more to hold.
A city is the mind of our heart's
desperate will to bring people together.
We build our separate ways.
Let's get together for a drink sometime.

V.

Some hearts are like towns, tough to leave—
a drawer in someone's kitchen you both used
to keep packs of mustard, soy sauce, chopsticks.
But I know a time will come soon
after Cooncoe's, at 3 A.M., when
everything on the highway goes quiet.
In my packed car driving east and south
I'll give my best to those brown waves, tennis shoes
and tires in The Monongahela. I will miss her deep-hole smells

when the lights go out in the house
of love. From the west
end of town a deep rumbling begins.
It's coming this way, building, the ground vibrates.
Thirteen motorcycles flow slowly by, moving east, just feet
from the bar. I look into Cooncoe's behind me.
Under the neon Stroh's at the window each pink face inside
is watching with terrible longing and just a little fear.
But we can't trade empty for empty—
those feral engines pumping all night long
in each gorgeous cycle, each a near-cougar
flickering through us.

Skill Set

Dark Matter

We forget the wolfman once wasn't. In church
he howls off-key during "Amazing Grace" and leaves
cleaned chicken bones in the collection plate
but no one looks over for someone they once knew.

Loneliness is the pure energy of love
dressed in rags, night after night of solo Midnight
Matinee, can after wasted Barbasol can.
It gets that way when life wears a jacket
with sleeves ending well before the wrists.

When the wolfman dreams
his paws twitch. The night is moonless.
At the grocer's, he fills his cart

with barely a basket's worth—
A gallon of whole milk.
Cough drops. Smoked pig bones.
Sometimes he sneaks a few grapes.

Space and Falling Fast

With so much glass on the heart's freeway
no one remembers Pandora was made from the earth itself.

She's what we had to take for fire, and some ways
are never paved. Even if the stars were made from our bodies, so many people

would say there's more evil than good in this world, and they
might be right. They'd say Pandora knew just what she was doing.

But not you. Not even when we knew the difference.
In all the fuss you reached back into her jar, and when you left

the bedroom for the den and we both knew
it would be for good, I washed my hands in the hottest water.

Confession of the Number Crunchers

After the shock and the grieving, a law
was passed which made it illegal
to write the number zero in a counter-clockwise circle.

A few scientists and a marketing systems analyst had determined
the country's ills would be reversed if all citizens agreed
upon only writing proper clockwise zeros. Not everyone agreed.

Not all of us thought that way about nothing, so a new
law was introduced:
The number one will now represent
what the number zero has always stood for. The number zero
will no longer be kept in circulation. There is nothing

to be further gained from nothing. No one
seemed shocked, and as there was nothing
tangible to grieve for, we voted, and got
on with our business of emptying this universe.

Friendly Fire

To make matters worse, someone built
an escalator eleven stories high
that went nowhere. Every day people
step on at the bottom, rise slowly

above the filled streets, and higher still above buildings
until they fall to a screaming death. At dawn,
each body is mysteriously buried before the great
escalator opens that morning. Soon, a warning is posted.
Flyers go out, town meetings fill, but all the proper forms

have been filed with the city long ago.
At night, a thick chain prevents unauthorized use.
The town kids hang out there in the parking lot.
Sometimes they duck under that chain, and sit and drink
on the first few steps of the dark.

Sooner or Later

The hats
are close
but backwards

not what
would Jesus
do, but who

wouldn't do
what Judas
did?

The First Root

takes hold, and once wound in, impossible to tell if it's borne
fruit or seed, so you crush one pod in your hand
to see—but the good yield doesn't come
for you. Like an ackee it's poisonous
 even ripe.

You thought, "It's true—I should have left the harvest
in the field." In the beginning,
the root takes hold, is fed with hunger
and watered with thirst. The flesh
grows in rings

from a center made of luck and lust—around the spine,
through the wing holes of the sacrum and sternum
filled with prayer. Soon the thing grows higher.
Up at first like green ligules, then spread
grossly, and fatter at top than bottom,

the head bursts—the stalk gives way to weight and weather.
Like shells neither prize nor product, we make love
there the best we can, and crush each other in
our thorn-torn palms, that first
root taking hold.

It's Not Me, It's Me

The desert island, and only room
for either truth or fact . . . can I have a minute?
But while I'm dwelling on preference
let me tell you a bit about Lucy Skilled.
First off, she was. Second, she knew it.
Third, so did David H., my one good friend.
Fourth, he knew I knew. Fifth, she knew
he knew I knew, and knew I knew
his knowing. More wine. Red. Quickly.

It's not the difference in definition
bogging me down—but truth comes
from fact, and sometimes fact from truth.
Does Lucy think of me at night? Probably not.
She doesn't even talk to me, but turns
her hips to David H., now an accountant.
How can a simple poem being honest
make a mark against Goldman-Sachs?
But David H. and I know it's much harder
to hide the heart's beat than to split hairs.
Fact or truth? Take it all back beneath
the cover of desire and mess it to hell until
our parts don't fit. They both could have been in bed
with me—scientists today tell us that's the truth,
the whole catalogue of our wildest facts crammed
in the back pocket of true love; you pull it out
and dust it off, try hard not to let those cats
out of their bags, but the lovers always know:
the hip-grind that can only have come
from great practice is not a skill one masters
in a vacuum.
               But is it not wonderful and right that truth
is just the place for getting good at telling lies?
Isn't fact wrapped up in a pretty black bow?

David does my taxes. Lucy makes his meals at six.
I turn my key in its lock like a jeweler opening an empty safe—

that's how it goes with the unattainable.
You pay your money. You take your pick—then wish
you'd picked what the other guy got. I don't hate
either of them, in fact, I'm more than a little pleased.

The plain truth is they're meant for one another.
And though I can't tell truth from fact, or even swap
their definitions, I have made peace and moved on.
Or at least I've moved on.
                              But you know I haven't—
the torches I carry may be the lynch mob
lights of loneliness, but at least here, in this blunt poem
I've tried to crawl up underneath it all. I'd have
better luck screwing myself if I could. Hell, maybe I just did.
There's something that'll get me off
once on the island, almanac in one hand, bible in the other,
pages carved out prison-style.

City Shy

We get to the top
of the roller coaster,
when I confess I have

a fear of heights. You look
at me with total indifference—as we
glide down the top hump, I scream myself awake.

Please be careful. I have a terrible sweet tooth
for revenge. And I watch a lot of TV.

Monday morning after the first lonely bed?
It's as if the sidewalks of love
have reached out and pulled

a shoelace loose. Twelve steps
later I'm flat on my face.
And there's no grace coming

to work with cement scrapes
on your slacks, that's the kind
of thing people notice. It doesn't

matter if I'm dressed to kill.
The Water Cooler Gang knows
I no longer know their secret sign—

someone's hidden my time card.
The blinds in my boss's office draw
closed when I walk by.
                         Now you
might think loveloss and loneliness
would mean for me a lot of couch time
and reflection. It's one but not the other, not
nostalgia, but diving from the burning
27th floor, an infant in each arm.
Maybe great fame from the sudden CIA

operative-mission that saves
Earth, or a relative whose will
dares me to spend so much money
I must be given more—

a playful trist that ends
when you see me cruise

up to the ten-thousandth year
high school reunion in Spite's Corvette
with three blondes on each arm, having won
the lottery, Nobel Peace Prize, and silver medal
in the 10,000 meter just last week at the end

of another loop-de-loop dream.
I knew this one-heart town
wasn't big enough for the both of us.

One on One

Those dogs that smell cancer?
For years I'll regret not finding them sooner.
What I'm wondering about their noses
I'll be wondering soon about loneliness:

Packhorse sniffing out an earthquake.
Roadkill digesting itself in the womb—

the stars mean nothing when broken inside us.
Below them, that beach just goes on down the coastline.
Every dark wavelet pulls away another bit.
I put my face in your black curls, and each strand is a thinning island
on the outer banks at midnight, the minerals there so hard
I'd swear I get just a whiff of fresh dirt and heaven.

Penguin Logic

The young ecologist couple, just back
from their first summer vacation
thinking of divorce, have crawled across
the permafrost to study The Emperors'

mating. Through binoculars on the frozen pleat
of thin land where ice gives way to sea
and food—after a winter of females on the hunt,
males on the nest—ten-thousand thousand penguins

waddle to each other. Sexually interchangeable
in their tuxes, a touch of beaks like brush strokes
takes away any real guess work.

Over the summer, tucked strangely in their hollow
beds, did they see one another in penguin dreams?
Were they worried about loving again
with 14,000 miles of Antarctic between them?

With patience, and a fine layer of fat, I'd crawl
back whole continents, for one last faceful of your hair
I'd pull the few hours of each day's sunlight
into fires made of luck and lust.

Jesse Waters' poems, stories and essays have appeared across the globe in such magazines as *Cimarron Review*, *Iowa Review*, *Magma*, *Story Quarterly* and others. He directs the Bowers Writers House at Elizabethtown College.

CPSIA information can be obtained at www.ICGtesting.com
Printed in the USA
LVOW07s1609171215

466935LV00001B/19/P